21st Century Skills **INNOVATION** Library

Swimming

by Stephen Timblin

Published in the United States of America by Cherry Lake Publishing
Ann Arbor, Michigan
www.cherrylakepublishing.com

Content Adviser: Thomas Sawyer, EdD, Professor of Recreation and Sport Management, Indiana State University

Design: The Design Lab

Photo Credits: Cover and page 3, ©Aflo Foto Agency/Alamy; page 4, ©Chad McDermott, used under license from Shutterstock, Inc.; page 6, ©iStockphoto.com/colleenbradley; pages 9, 22, 26, and 28, ©AP Photo; page 10, ©AP Photo/Steve Holland; page 13, ©iStockphoto.com/tobntno; page 14, ©Sean Nel, used under license from Shutterstock, Inc.; page 17, ©iStockphoto.com/ShaneKato; page 18, ©Brian Chase, used under license from Shutterstock, Inc.; page 19, ©AP Photo/Kyle Ericson; page 20, ©H. Mark Weidman Photography/Alamy; page 25, ©AP Photo/USPS; page 27, ©AP Photo/AMC

Library of Congress Cataloging-in-Publication Data
Timblin, Stephen.
 Swimming / by Stephen Timblin.
    p. cm.–(Innovation in sports)
 Includes index.
 ISBN-13: 978-1-60279-258-6
 ISBN-10: 1-60279-258-5
 1. Swimming–Juvenile literature. I. Title. II. Series.
 GV837.6.T56 2009
 797.21–dc22   2008002046

*Cherry Lake Publishing would like to acknowledge the work of
The Partnership for 21st Century Skills.
Please visit* www.21stcenturyskills.org *for more information.*

CONTENTS

INNOVATION IN SPORTS

CHAPTER ONE

The Story of Swimming

In the world of competitive swimming, where records are made to be broken, every second counts.

In the world of competitive swimming, records are made to be broken. Even five years is considered a long time for a world record to stay unbroken. If you look back at old record times, modern swimmers aren't just beating those records—they're shattering them! Back in 1915, the best time for the 200-meter women's freestyle was 2:56 (2 minutes and 56 seconds). That mark has been broken dozens of times since then. Today, that record, held by France's Laure Manaudou, stands at just over 1:55—a full minute faster!

Why is it that today's swimmers are faster than the swimmers of the past? And why is it that today's records will likely be shattered in the near future? Swimming seems like a simple activity. But over time there have been innovations in just about every aspect of the sport. To explore how these innovations have led to faster swimmers, let's look at the history of swimming.

Swimming is one of the oldest sports on Earth. The earliest known civilizations were built near water. **Archaeologists** in Egypt have uncovered **hieroglyphics** dating back 5,000 years that show people swimming. Drawings from ancient Greece show men paddling through water. And in ancient Rome, swimming was part of a student's education. Rome was also known for its public bathhouses. These were places where citizens could swim and bathe.

Japan also has a rich history of swimming. Races were held as early as the first century BCE. By the 1600s, a Japanese law required that all students learn how to swim in school. Schools started competing against one another in nationally organized races.

Modern competitive swimming got its start in England. The city of Liverpool opened the first "swimming bath" in 1828. Swimming contests soon

Swimming has been a form of sport and recreation for centuries. The Roman Empire built public baths all over Europe, including England.

followed. In 1837, the first known swimming organization was formed in London. Other organizations began soon after, each hosting different swimming competitions.

The most widely used swimming **stroke** at that time was the breaststroke. In 1844, a group of Native

Americans was invited to London to compete in a contest. This group stunned crowds by beating other racers using a never-before-seen overhand style. This stroke style looked a lot like today's freestyle stroke.

Serious international competitions started when the modern Olympics kicked off in Athens, Greece, in 1896. The games included four swimming events, all held on the same day. Nearly 20,000 spectators watched 19 swimmers from 4 different countries compete.

To see how far swimming has come, take a quick look at the 2004 Summer Olympics in Athens. The 2004 games featured 32 different races and a lot more swimmers.

CHAPTER TWO

Pools and Rules

If you close your eyes and think about a swim meet, you probably aren't thinking about waves, underwater **obstacles**, and dirty water. But if you lived 100 years ago, you'd think just that. That's because the earliest swimming events weren't held in pools. Instead, they took place in open water—oceans, seas, rivers, and lakes.

At the 1896 Olympics in Athens, the swimming events were held in the salty Mediterranean Sea. At the 1900 Olympics in Paris, swimmers had to dive into the muddy waters of the Seine River. It wasn't until the 1908 Olympics in London that the first pool was used. But even then, it wasn't what you'd expect. The organizers built a giant water tank located inside the main stadium. Swimmers complained that they couldn't see anything in the nearly black water due to the lack of lighting.

Hungarian Alfred Hajos became the first modern Olympic swimming champion at the 1896 Olympics in Athens, Greece.

In those days, too, the host countries held some events that seem strange by today's standards. For example, the 1900 Olympics included a 200-meter swimming obstacle course. It had swimmers climbing over poles and swimming under a row of boats. There was even an underwater swimming competition that timed who could hold his breath the longest!

Since 1908, FINA has been the official governing organization for international swimming events, including water polo.

Without a standard list of events and rules, it was becoming impossible to declare true champions. After the 1908 Olympics, representatives from eight European countries came together to fix this problem. They created the first international swimming organization, named the Fédération Internationale de Natation (FINA). FINA runs the most important world championships in swimming, diving, synchronized swimming, water polo, and open water swimming. It remains the governing body of international competitive swimming and determines what the rules are.

By the 1920s, FINA made sure that the top swimming events were held in standardized pools. Many innovative changes have been made to these pools over the years. Regulation-sized pools now have buffer lanes and lane markers. These innovations keep waves to a minimum so they don't distract swimmers. These regulation pools help in organizing standard events, and give swimmers a consistent "field" to practice in.

FINA had a lot of work to do to clean up the record books. One problem was that races in some events were measured in yards while others used meters. By 1969, FINA made sure that all races and records were recorded only in meters.

Learning & Innovation Skills

It seems hard to believe that swimming events used to be held in oceans and rivers. But if you were at the first Olympic Games way back in 1896, it would have seemed just as crazy to think that in the future, athletes would compete in swimming pools.

Imagine that it is your job in the early 1900s to convince a skeptical public that pools are the wave of the future. How do you convince people that you are right? You could start by mentioning the fact that swimmers in pools wouldn't have to worry about sharks or dangerous river currents. What other points would you make to convince people that your pool plan was a good one?

CHAPTER THREE

Suit Yourself

In ancient times, the only thing a person needed to go swimming was water. Swimming caps, goggles, and even bathing suits weren't used. That's right—the only suit people swam in was their birthday suit!

In the early 1800s, the first swimming **garments** were created. These swimsuits were designed with modesty in mind. Women's swimsuits at this time were long dresses that covered everything from their necks down to their ankles. Some swimsuits even had weights at the bottom to make sure wind or water wouldn't lift them up! Men's suits didn't cover quite as much, but they looked a lot like long underwear.

By the start of the 1900s, styles began to change. People began feeling less worried about showing their body in public. Swimsuits started to shrink. The bottom

Swimsuits of the past covered more of the body than they do today. This style of suit is from the 1920s.

of men's bathing suits reached only to the knee. Women's swimsuits allowed the sun to hit their legs below the knee and their entire arms. Swimming was much easier in such a suit. These smaller suits allowed swimmers to swim even faster than before. It's no **coincidence** that women started entering swimming competitions soon after their swimsuits got smaller.

Today's lightweight caps and goggles help swimmers move faster through the water.

As competitive swimming grew in popularity, swimsuits shrank even more. In 1914, Alexander MacRae created the Speedo swimwear company on Bondi Beach near Sydney, Australia. Speedo was one of the first companies to make suits for pro swimmers. Speedo has since become a global success by constantly working to come up with better, faster swimsuits. Speedo's smaller, tight-fitting swimsuits made from lightweight materials such as Lycra and nylon are more than just stylish. They are a huge reason why race times are better now. Smaller swimsuits help swimmers cut through the water faster and with less **drag**. The old, bulky swimwear acted like mini-parachutes that held swimmers back as they tried to move forward. Most older swimsuits were made of wool. They got **waterlogged** and weighed swimmers down.

Another cause of drag was hair. Then someone came up with the idea of a tight-fitting swim cap. This reduced the slowing effect of hair on the head. But some racers decided they wanted to do something about the drag caused by other body hair. So they started wearing full-length bodysuits to help cut down on drag caused by leg and arm hair. Other swimmers have attacked the problem in a different way. They simply shave off their body hair. Shaving your entire body may seem like a lot of trouble to save a tenth of second. But a tenth of a

21st Century Content

Looking to get an edge on their competitors, the experts at Speedo recently studied one of the world's fastest swimmers—sharks! The company spent four years on this top-secret project. The designers learned that the shape of a shark's skin changes across its body, helping it flow through water faster with less resistance. The end result was the Fastskin FSII series of bodysuits. The company thinks these bodysuits could change competitive swimwear forever. If you're hoping to try one out, you'd better start saving up. This full-body version of a swimsuit can cost as much as $400!

second can mean the difference between winning and coming in fourth place.

Another innovation solved a problem swimmers were having. Swimmers suffered from sore, red eyes because of the chemicals used to keep swimming pools clean. The solution? Goggles started being worn in the late 1960s to protect swimmers' eyes.

CHAPTER FOUR

Training for Success

A professional female swimmer flies out of the water as she does the butterfly stroke. Training takes time and a lot of energy.

Cool-looking swimsuits and goggles aren't the only innovations that help swimmers beat records. World-class swimmers will tell you that the difference between first and last place is training. Let's take a look at how innovative training techniques have led to the most dramatic improvements in swimming.

Originally, people trained for lifesaving purposes. It didn't really matter how you swam as long as you could make it through the water. As competitions started, swimmers began training to improve both their **endurance** and their strokes. Swimmers would swim and swim, until their muscles gave out.

The great James "Doc" Counsilman was one of the first coaches to figure out that training like that actually caused more harm than good. Pushing yourself too hard creates a high possibility of injury and overall muscle

During training, swimmers must rest between sets of laps to build strength and avoid injury.

fatigue. Today, **interval** training is the most popular training method. Instead of swimming nonstop, swimmers go a set distance, with breaks in between. Sometimes swimmers swim a single lap as hard as possible and then

Coach, scientist, and author James "Doc" Counsilman used underwater photography to improve his swimmers' strokes.

rest before repeating the distance 10 more times. Other times, they swim 20 laps before taking a short break and then repeat the distance a few more times.

Counsilman brought a scientist's perspective to the sport of swimming. He studied the principles of physics and used them to perfect stroke techniques. In 1968, he wrote *The Science of Swimming*, a book that remains a classic to this day. He was also one of the first coaches to use underwater photography to study swimmers' strokes. He realized that a stroke might look fine from above, but imperfections might be seen if observed from another perspective.

Some experts think that the biggest reason swimmers' times have improved so much is that today's swimmers turn faster at the end of each lap. For example, freestyle swimmers nowadays all use a flip turn, also called a somersault, or tumble turn, in competition. When approaching a wall, swimmers make an underwater somersault, kicking back off the wall to propel forward again. Julian "Tex" Robertson, a legendary swimming coach at the University of Texas, was the innovator of this turn. Robertson was a competitive swimmer as

The aquatic stadium is filled at the 1936 Summer Olympics in Berlin, Germany. Adolph Kiefer won a gold medal here using an underwater somersault at the end of each lap.

well as a coach. He realized that by flipping and pushing off the wall, swimmers could turn much more quickly than by simply swimming all the way to the pool's end.

Robertson's new flip turn was a swimming sensation when the athletes he trained used it at the 1936 Olympics. His pupil, Adolph Kiefer, won a gold medal thanks to the revolutionary technique!

CHAPTER FIVE

Swimming Superstars

The history of swimming is full of stories about extraordinary athletes, fierce competitors, and outstanding innovators. The following four individuals represent the finest superstars of swimming.

Duke Kahanamoku

Born in 1890, Hawaii's Duke Kahanamoku was one of the first swimmers to become famous worldwide. Raised in Honolulu, swimming was a part of his daily life. Most of his playmates simply swam for fun, but a determined Kahanamoku turned his swimming skills into a successful career. By training hard and creating a new style of kicking motion, he became the best freestyle swimmer of his time. He broke his first swimming world record in 1911. He beat the previous freestyle mark for a

Life & Career Skills

Olympic gold medalist Duke Kahanamoku (1890–1968) could have relaxed and enjoyed life by the beach in Hawaii between swimming competitions. Instead, the innovative thinker turned one of his favorite hobbies, surfing, into a sport famous around the world. Few people outside of Hawaii had even heard of surfing before Kahanamoku came along. He started giving surfing demonstrations in places such as Australia and California. As a result, the sport quickly became a worldwide hit. Considered the "father of surfing," Duke was the first athlete to be inducted into both the Swimming Hall of Fame and the Surfing Hall of Fame. Today, a statue of Duke standing with a surfboard overlooks Honolulu's buzzing Waikiki Beach.

100-yard (91 m) race by 4 seconds. But the Amateur Athletic Union refused to believe the time. Instead of letting that get him down, the upbeat Kahanamoku proved his doubters wrong. He won a gold medal in the 100-meter freestyle at the 1912 Olympics.

After his first Summer Olympics, the always-smiling Hawaiian became a worldwide celebrity by touring the globe. He won two more gold medals at the 1920 Olympics. His final Olympics in 1924 was a family affair. Duke won the silver in the 100-meter freestyle, and his brother Samuel won the bronze.

Johnny Weissmuller

Born in Europe in 1904, Johnny Weissmuller moved to America before his first birthday. By 1928, he had won 5 Olympic gold medals, set 67 world records, and won 52 U.S. National

USA 34

DUKE KAHANAMOKU

2002

In 2002, the U.S. Postal Service honored swimmer and surfer Duke Kahanamoku for his achievements.

Championships. In fact, he never lost a single race in his entire amateur swimming career! What's most interesting about Weissmuller's story is what he did after retiring from competitive swimming. Instead of giving up on his sport, he figured out a way to use his swimming skills in a new career as a movie star. He played the role of

Johnny Weissmuller was one of history's greatest male swimmers. His speed, strength, and grace in the water awed his fans.

Tarzan in a dozen movies, each one filled with action-packed swimming scenes that audiences loved. The Tarzan movies helped turn Weissmuller into a worldwide superstar. He ended up earning the actor's version of a gold medal—a star on the Hollywood Walk of Fame.

Lynne Cox

Do you complain that your local pool is too cold early in the morning? If so, you'll turn blue just thinking about long-distance swimmer Lynne Cox. Born in 1957, she has spent her life tackling swimming challenges

Lynne Cox is the first woman to swim many dangerous waters around the world in record time. In 1974, at the age of 18, Cox prepares to swim across Cook Strait in New Zealand.

that seem impossible—until she completes them! Cox was 15 years old when she broke the world record for swimming across the English Channel, a 10-hour swim through dangerous waters. She's also the first person to ever swim around Cape Point in South Africa through shark-filled waters!

One of her recent quests is perhaps the most amazing swim of all. In 2002, Cox became the first person to ever complete a 1.2-mile (2 km) swim in Antarctica. Most people couldn't survive 5 minutes in water that cold. By following her own one-of-a-kind cold-water training program since she was a child, she was able to spend close to 30 minutes swimming in nearly frozen waters, wearing just a regular bathing suit!

Life & Career Skills

In 2004, Michael Phelps was the first American to win eight medals at one Olympic Games. At the same Olympics, he became the first swimmer in history to qualify in six individual events. The secret to Phelps's amazing success is training as hard as he possibly can to stay on top. "If you don't put the work in, you can't really expect to get much out of it," says Michael. "I'm more than willing to put the work in so I'm swimming fast at the end of the year." Phelps's work ethic and athleticism will help him continue to shatter swimming records for years to come.

Glossary

archaeologists (ar-kee-OL-uh-jists) people who study objects from the past to understand how people lived

coincidence (koh-IN-si-duhnss) something that happens by chance in a surprising way

drag (DRAG) something that restricts or limits motion

endurance (en-DUR-uhnss) the ability to continue an activity for a long time

fatigue (fuh-TEEG) exhaustion or tiredness

garments (GAR-muhnts) clothing

hieroglyphics (hye-ruh-GLIF-iks) the ancient Egyptian alphabet, which used pictures instead of letters

interval (IN-tur-vuhl) a space of time between events

obstacles (OB-stuh-kuhlz) things that get in the way of the path ahead

skeptical (SKEP-tuh-kuhl) to have doubt about something

stroke (STROHK) a series of repeated movements

undaunted (uhn-DAWN-tid) to remain undiscouraged and show no fear

waterlogged (WAW-tur-logd) to be filled or soaked with water

For More Information

BOOKS

Crowe, Ellie, and Richard Waldrep (illustrator). *Surfer of the Century: The Life of Duke Kahanamoku*. New York: Lee and Low Books, 2007.

Kehm, Greg. *Olympic Swimming and Diving*. New York: Rosen Central Publishing, 2007.

Sapet, Kerrily. *Michael Phelps*. Greensboro, NC: Morgan Reynolds Publishing, 2008.

WEB SITES

FINA
http://fina.org
The best place to look online for the latest swimming records, upcoming championship events, and videos of past races

Michael Phelps
www.michaelphelps.com
The official site of the young American swimming sensation

USA Swimming
www.usaswimming.org
Check in for tips on improving your swimming, and read quick biographies of the U.S. swim team's top athletes

Index

About the Author

Stephen Timblin is a longtime writer and all-around sports nut. He lives with his lovely wife near Detroit, Michigan, and spends his summers swimming in many of the nearby lakes. The greatest swimmer he knows is his father-in-law, Lino, who once swam the Naples-to-Capri race in Italy, a distance of just more than 22 miles!